RYE FREE READING ROOM

GOBLIN SHARK

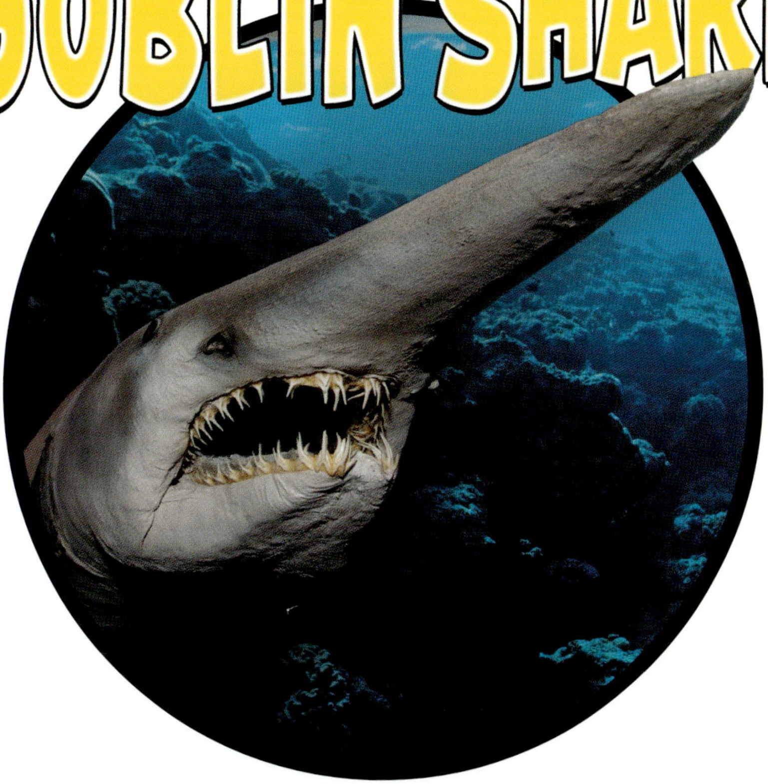

By Rachel Rose

Consultant: Erin McCombs
Educator, Aquarium of the Pacific

Minneapolis, Minnesota

Credits

Cover and title page, © Kelvin Aitken/Alamy, © NOPPHARAT7824/Shutterstock, © creativesunday/Shutterstock; 3, © nabil refaat/Shutterstock; 4-5, © Pally/Alamy; 6-7, © Kelvin Aitken/Alamy; 8, © Sport08/Shutterstock; 8-9, © David Shen/BluepPlanetArchive; 10-11, © Makoto Hirose/BluepPlanetArchive; 12-13, © Paulo de Oliveira/biosphoto; 14-15, © Makoto Hirose/BluepPlanetArchive; 16-17, © David Shen/BluepPlanetArchive; 18-19, © Pally/Alamy; 20-21, © Makoto Hirose/BluepPlanetArchive; 22, © Marko Steffensen/Alamy; 22-23, © nabil refaat/Shutterstock; 24, © nabil refaat/Shutterstock.

President: Jen Jenson
Director of Product Development: Spencer Brinker
Senior Editor: Allison Juda
Associate Editor: Charly Haley
Designer: Colin O'Dea

Library of Congress Cataloging-in-Publication Data

Names: Rose, Rachel, 1968- author.
Title: Goblin shark / Rachel Rose.
Description: Minneapolis, Minnesota : Bearport Publishing Company, [2022] | Series: Shark shock! | Includes bibliographical references and index.
Identifiers: LCCN 2021030936 (print) | LCCN 2021030937 (ebook) | ISBN 9781636915302 (library binding) | ISBN 9781636915395 (paperback) | ISBN 9781636915487 (ebook)
Subjects: LCSH: Goblin shark--Juvenile literature.
Classification: LCC QL638.95.M58 R67 2022 (print) | LCC QL638.95.M58 (ebook) | DDC 597.3/3--dc23
LC record available at https://lccn.loc.gov/2021030936
LC ebook record available at https://lccn.loc.gov/2021030937

Copyright © 2022 Bearport Publishing Company. All rights reserved. No part of this publication may be reproduced in whole or in part, stored in any retrieval system, or transmitted in any form or by any means, electronic, mechanical, photocopying, recording, or otherwise, without written permission from the publisher.

For more information, write to Bearport Publishing, 5357 Penn Avenue South, Minneapolis, MN 55419. Printed in the United States of America.

CONTENTS

Open Wide............................... 4
Deep Dive 6
A Shark Like No Other 8
Slow Swimmers 10
Snappy Speed 12
Sixth Sense 14
Terrifying Teeth 16
Hard to Reach......................... 18
Many Mysteries 20

More about Goblin Sharks 22
Glossary............................... 23
Index.................................. 24
Read More............................. 24
Learn More Online 24
About the Author...................... 24

Open Wide

It's dark deep in the ocean where a goblin shark waits for its next meal. It barely moves until a fish swims close by. Then, the goblin shark shoots its jaw forward and opens wide. It traps the fish in its mouth and then quickly snaps its jaw back into place. Score!

A goblin shark moves its jaw out from its head like a **slingshot** to catch passing **prey**.

Deep Dive

These freaky fish are no strangers to the dark depths. Goblin sharks live mostly in the deep waters of the Atlantic, Indian, and Pacific Oceans. In fact, they can swim almost a mile (1.6 km) below the waves.

Goblin sharks are rarely seen because they live so far down in the ocean.

GOBLIN SHARKS AROUND THE WORLD

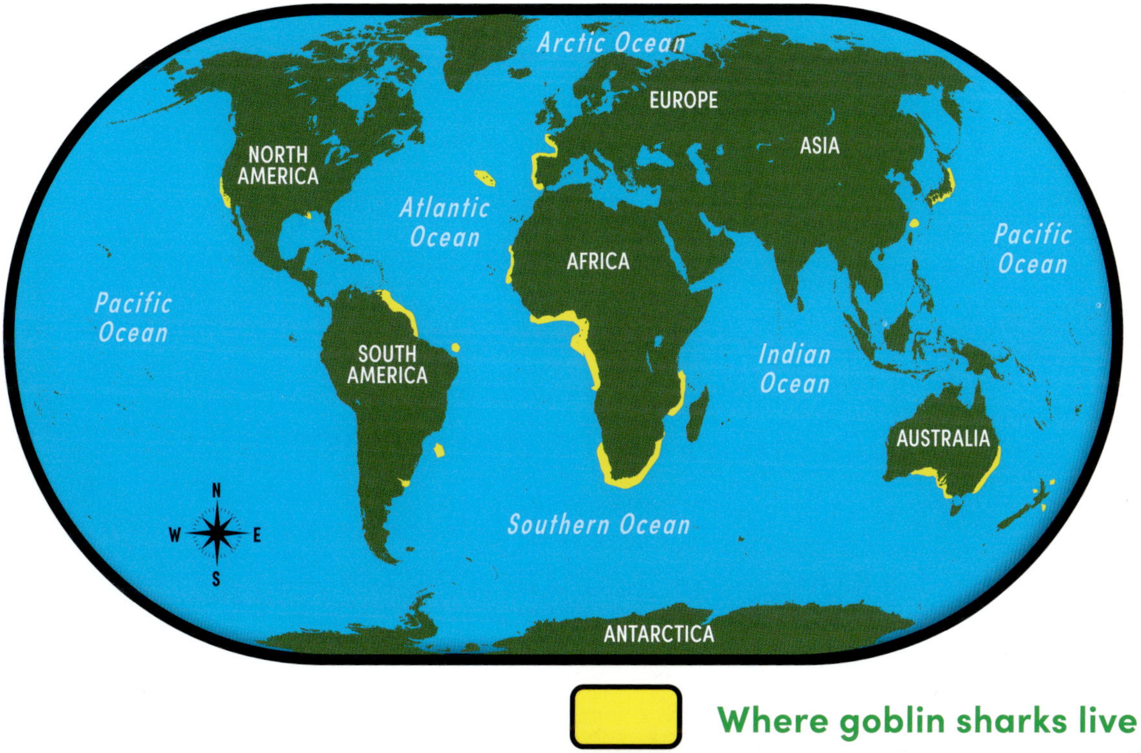

■ **Where goblin sharks live**

A Shark Like No Other

Goblin sharks cut through the water point-first. Their superlong noses stick out far past their jaws below. These pointed noses even earned the sharks their name. They reminded scientists of the long, sharp noses on **mythical** goblins.

A goblin

Another thing that sets these sharks apart is their see-through skin. It can make them look pink because you can see their blood below.

> Goblin sharks have tiny eyes. They don't need them deep in the dark ocean.

Slow Swimmers

Goblin sharks have big, **flabby** bodies. Although they can grow about 12 feet (3.7 m) long—as long as a small car—they do not have much **muscle**. These sharks have small fins and tails that are more bendy than strong. Because of all of these things, goblin sharks are not fast swimmers.

Goblin sharks can weigh up to 460 pounds (200 kg).

Snappy Speed

Luckily, when they are hunting, goblin sharks don't need to rely on swimming speed. They are speedy in another way—with their mouths! Goblin sharks' jaws shoot out of their mouths at a speed of 10 ft (3 m) per second to catch their prey. Once they have grabbed the tasty treat, their jaws quickly snap back in place.

A goblin shark's jaw moves even faster than a cobra snake can strike.

Sixth Sense

A goblin shark's hunting skills are helped by having an extra sense. Special **cells** in its snout can sense the **electrical signals** of other sea creatures. This means the shark can find prey even without being able to see very far in the dark depths.

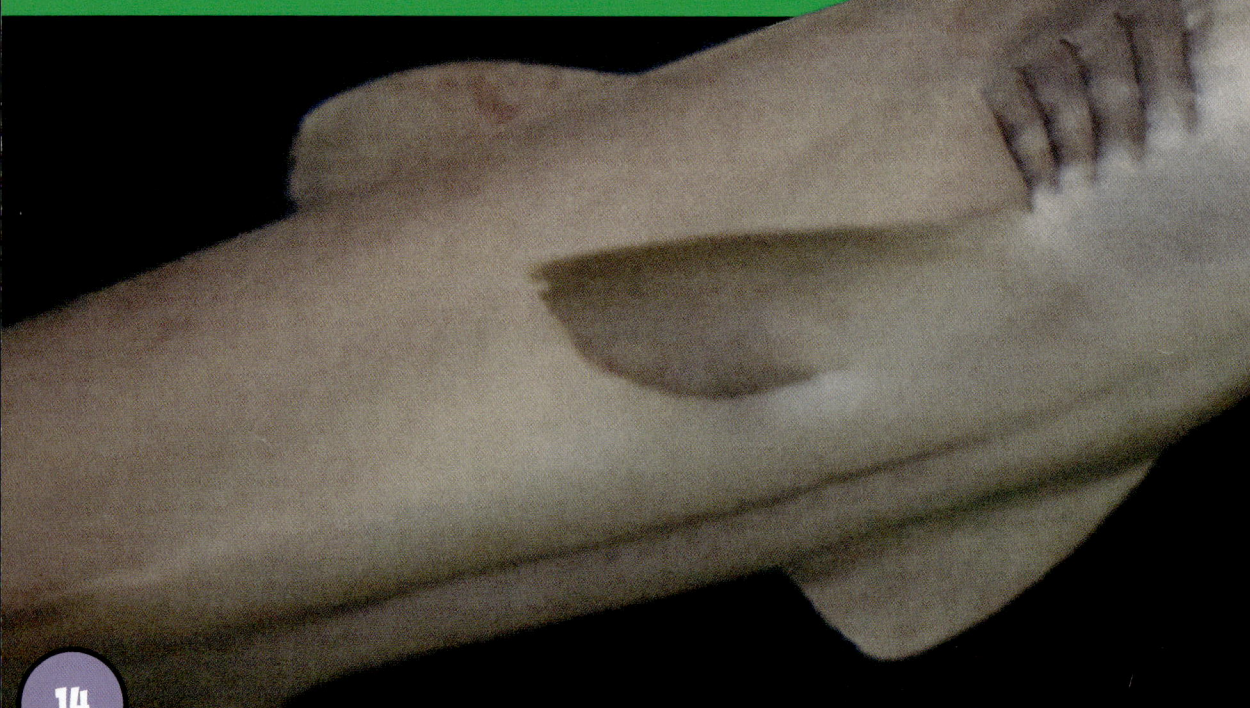

Every animal gives out waves of electricity. Very few animals can feel the electricity, but all sharks can!

Terrifying Teeth

What do these great hunters eat? Goblin sharks feed mostly on bony fish, squid, octopuses, and crabs.

The sharks have several kinds of teeth. At the front of their mouths, sharp, pointy teeth help goblin sharks snag their prey. Then, wide and flat back teeth crush hard bones and shells.

> Some of a goblin shark's teeth are curved backward. They keep prey from trying to swim out of the shark's mouth.

Hard to Reach

Goblin sharks have very few **predators**. The toothy, slow swimmers are most likely to be hunted by other sharks, such as blue sharks.

But unlike many other kinds of sharks, goblin sharks are mostly safe from fishing humans. Their deep, watery homes make goblin sharks hard to reach.

Most goblin sharks that have been caught were found off the coast of Japan.

Many Mysteries

Because they live mostly out of sight, much about goblin sharks is still a mystery. Although scientists haven't gotten close enough to study them, they think that goblin sharks give birth to live babies. But as soon as they are born, the babies disappear into the dark waters just like their parents.

More about Goblin Sharks

Goblin sharks are sometimes called elfin sharks. Mythical elves have long noses, too.

It is believed that goblin sharks use their long snouts to poke around for food.

Because goblin sharks swim in such deep waters, humans are rarely in any danger from these sharks.

Goblin sharks have been around for 125 million years.

The first goblin shark was discovered off the coast of Japan in 1897.

Glossary

cells basic, very tiny parts of a person, animal, or plant

electrical signals information in the form of weak electricity surrounding some creatures

flabby not hard or firm

muscle a part of the body that is used to cause movement

mythical related to a set of stories, folklore, or beliefs of a particular group or culture

predators animals that hunt and kill other animals for food

prey animals that are hunted and eaten by other animals

slingshot a Y-shaped stick with an elastic band attached for shooting small stones

Index

cells 14
food 22
humans 18, 22
hunting 12, 14, 16, 18
jaw 4–5, 8, 12–13, 16
oceans 4, 6–7, 9
predator 18
prey 5, 12, 14, 16
snouts 14, 22
teeth 16, 18

Read More

Alderman, Christine Thomas. *Goblin Sharks (Swimming With Sharks)*. Mankato, MN: Black Rabbit Books, 2020.

Hansen, Grace. *Goblin Sharks (Spooky Animals)*. Minneapolis: Abdo Kids, 2021.

Learn More Online

1. Go to www.factsurfer.com or scan the QR code below.
2. Enter "Goblin Shark" into the search box.
3. Click on the cover of this book to see a list of websites.

About the Author

Rachel Rose lives in California. She swims in the ocean every day, and she sees plenty of seals—but she hasn't seen a shark yet!

RYE FREE READING ROOM
1061 BOSTON POST ROAD
RYE NEW YORK 10580
(914) 967-0480

JUN 0 1 2022